MOCKTALES

MIXOLOGY OF LIFE - SERVED 'SHAKEN' AND 'STIRRED'

THE BARTENDING POET

Dedicated to all the "unknowns" who make a massive contribution to the world but we never know their name

Contents

Contents

Contents

Contents

I
Courage

Courage is one thing that can't be measured
It takes seconds or years to find it is there
Most people live in fear and forget their strength
It takes strength to swim against the tide and persevere

So, while you are confused and contemplating
Think of the time when you said while people tried
silencing
While you are looking for an answer for this question
Courage itself is a question of asking when Noone is
answering

II

Chance

I was confused with all the messages
Noise they made to convince they want my welfare
I can't figure out what was said in the passages
In books of love and law, I just wanted to avoid the
fanfare

Now, I have figured it out, I have to play with the "Choice"
What I can say and where I use my silence
I have created a web of simple truth, knit with subtle
lies
Let them choose what they want, I let the "chance" do its
dance

III

Only You

You got to believe yourself
You got to aim for the stars
You got to strive for a better self
You got to change the worlds afar

You got to take the step today
You got to make this earth a better place
You got to look at the sky and gleam
You got to keep the promise that you made to your
dreams

You got to fill the forms and strive
You got to make a dent and strike
You got to fight for everyone's sake
You got to rise from my ashes laid bare

IV

Can We?

Can we Rise up to the Occasion?
Can we Avoid some Distractions?
Can we Bend our Ego?
Can we Break some Silences?
Can we Right our Evils?
Can we Leave some Battles?

V

Superhero

One can be Batman without the Money
One can be Spiderman without the Webbing
All it takes is the will to make a Difference
Else anyone can find excuses, they are Plenty

VI

No Point

I write so that someone can read
I read so that someone can write
I don't essentially have a purpose
I just transfer what I surmise

VII

Your Worth

How can you call yourself a failure
If you made someone smile
How can you call yourself spineless
If you stood against the lies

How can you call yourself useless
If you acted instead of giving advice
How can you call yourself worthless
If you valued kindness over price

VIII

Compromise

Can you teach me what is left?
Can you learn what is right?
Can we at least talk and digest?
The differences and break the ice

IX

Hope

You think I fight to Win?
You think I want to be a King?
You think I want to be godly dressed?
My struggle is the hope, a message I only cared

X
Fight Right

You might have to walk alone
You might have to fight on your own
Sometimes destiny puts you on an edge
To decide what's right and who's wrong

So keep your head high and heart steady
Fight the ones who are vile and greedy
Doesn't matter if they're your family or enemy
Sometimes the differences fade away quickly

XI

Assumptions

Just because I am nice
Doesn't mean I don't know how to fight
Just because I avoid fight
Doesn't mean I won't shout the battle cry
Just because I cry
Doesn't mean I don't know war tactics and strategy
Just because I am kind
Doesn't mean I will be merciful against the demons
outside

XII

Beacon

Walk alone if you can't find anyone
Talk to yourself if you can't find an audience
Love yourself if you find selfishness in everyone
Hope at least to keep alive your conscience

World's disdain has brought you pain
Become a symbol for at least someone
Of Compassion to all, without any condition
Live is short, you can sometimes take an absence

XIII
New Breed

Raise your boys to be brave
Raise your girls to be brave
Raise anyone you want to save
Like your own child and make them brave

World will need a new breed
Of men and women in same creed
To fight the battle on every sphere
The lines have gone, the cursors are here

XIV
Wish For You

I haven't written for you for long
I thought I was writing a song
I hope you don't think I wrote for myself
I hope you see that I see love in your own self

&

I have missed so many times
To kiss you on the cheek and speak in Rhymes
I know I hear less, and talk a lot
I am listening, just sometimes I get lost

&

I will try to better myself
To be the love and friend you want
I know you need more from me
I will deliver as time has come

&

I wish I can make you a dream
That you dreamt but didn't realize

THE BARTENDING POET

I wish I can take you home
That's your own and a bit of mine

XV
Undefeatable

My soul is not for Sale
You sold yours for ego's sake
There are things that I make
Poems and Songs, that you can't take

So why do you think you stand a chance
Against a person who plays in a war
So why you think you have a choice
Against a person who fights with a voice

XVI

It's Coming

I know it's hard, but don't you worry
People have ego, it's hard to say sorry
You know you are different, and you do try
People's indifference is the reason that you cry

But hold on, tide will turn
Time will change, a fire will burn
With every step, you will realize
A million lives changed, with your smile

XVII

Blind Players

Why play against the one who laid the boundaries and the
rules
Why challenge the one who made the sixty-four squares
and painted in two
What CHANCE you have to win the battle
His CHOICE has already made you player in the game

XVIII
Warrior

I had the excuses said by the best
I had the means laid by the rest
I had the Chance to destroy everyone
I Chose to avoid conflict to love someone

But just because I don't like fights
Doesn't mean I won't declare war to defend honour
Just because I speak only in the language of Kindness
Doesn't mean that I won't speak in law, science and
religion, that evil understands

XIX

Hypokraitism

There is a religion I follow
It doesn't have any prophet
Everyone is also with me
Without realizing they also believe

Hypocrisy is a human nature
More basic than they admit
You might won't even recognize
What you despise, you also commit

XX

Beware

Beware of "Educated Illiterates"
They like "likes" even if its lies
They comment even overhead it flies
They share "views" with closed eyes

They support causes without reasons
They "reason" without any supporting evidence
They "believe" their "science"
They rationalize death of conscience

XXI
Doesn't Make Sense

I have to write in Rhymes
Because no one listens to Reasons
I have to make a melody
Because people ignore tragedy

I post on social media
That's the only thing people care
They will let a person die
To keep their mobile alive

XXII

First Think

How can you call someone Success or Failure
If you don't even know the question paper
How can you call someone Less worthy or Useless
If you don't even know what "worth" actually means

൭

Before you pass judgement on someone
Do you think you are capable to be on the seat of a
judge
Before you call someone incapable
Do you think you are even capable to think

XXIII

Life Source

I will fall, it's in my destiny
Just like water, before it turns to stream
It's not how many times earth stops me
Life on it can't survive without me

XXIV

Too Slow to Help

Don't delay the Justice
Don't let the Victim suffer more
Your Time is running out
And my vengeance will come in many forms

XXV
Salmon's Will

I don't know why they don't teach about Salmon
Their will and persistence to keep carrying on
Starting from a spring and end up in an Ocean
It travels back upwards the mountains, defying gravity,
to keep life moving on

XXVI
Step of Life

Once you consider yourself better than the rest
You just change prison, but never see the bars

&

Freedom is accepting we are nothing while creating
things during existence, and end up in nothingness while
the things we created will follow the same path

&

There is no purpose. The next step for an embryo is birth,
the next step for the old body is death

&

So, keep taking steps, keep flowing through space and time
and don't worry about your name, fame, money or mark

XXVII

Silent Reveals

When silence speaks, society can't turn down the truth
It's an art that only few have mastered on their own
To make people shut up and listen carefully
It's important to make your words clear, and silence,
quite heavy

XXVIII
Adjust Culture

Husband violent but wife should "Adjust"
Father beats but son should "Adjust"
Mother-in-law abuses but daughter-in law should
"Adjust"
Son throws out mother, society "Adjusts"
Daughter beaten but parents say "Adjust"
Unreasonable does anything, Reasonable is told "Adjust"
Don't worry, it will be "Just" to force you to also "Adjust"

XXIX
Weather the Storm

Let us try one more time
Dreams might turn sublime
There might be some sunshine
A choice to live and a chance to smile

The night has been long, after all
There might be a heavy withdrawal
Sometimes hailstorms follow rainfall
Wait till weather clears, to carry on

XXX

It's Done

Run and hide, it's all done
It's no longer your chance to run
This world and people's lives
You need to be eradicated from this earth

My vengeance won't be swift
It will cut slowly and down the bone
My wrath will annihilate what you built
Now pray to your symbols and stones

XXXI

Minimise to Control

Giving excuses for the "wrong"
Convincing "right" to move on
It's a daily injustice that goes on
"Normalization of crime" to keep the tag of "norm"

The society never dares to face the bad
It silences the ones who even dare to fight
Not because they are afraid or powerless
They hide behind their twisted morals for their need to
control

XXXII

Kind Cure

The words are quite valuable
But actions have their significance
It's easier to preach lessons
Than practice and teach to the young ones

Earning a living is easier, living with principle is difficult
Yearning for desires is usual, controlling is unnatural
It's comfortable to conform to the norms, even wrong
But standing alone, not everyone is capable

So be kind to each other
World is already losing humanity
Your love and compassion is needed
To preserve, whatever is left of sanity

XXXIII
Poetic Reality

I have written more than a million words
Think how many I have read

&

I have fought a thousand battles
Think how many I have avoided

&

I have saved a hundred people
Think how many I have disappointed

&

I have published countless poems
Think how many still need an end

XXXIV
Defend

A new start, a new vision
No need to ask permission
A small step in right direction
No reason to give an explanation

I will make my way like a river
I will create a civilization nearby
I will nurture the kids in the rain
I will drown the demons that prey

It's not my nature to seek conflict
But I won't back down from a fight
To defend the defenceless in the midst
I promise to protect with all my might

XXXV

Enlightenment

From equations of non-linear dynamics in Mathematics
From postulates of quantum physics
From findings in neuroscience
And from verses of Bhagvad Geeta

I ventured down many paths
I stumbled upon many solutions
Only conclusion that I got
It's better to accept truth than live in an illusion

XXXVI

The Journey

Do smile because world is small
Do try because it's worth the crawl
Who said happiness is the ultimate goal
An interesting journey and good mate is what we need
after all

XXXVII

Manipulate the Man

Illusion of Power is a subtle art
Offer a man free will and praise his heart
Elevate him in his own mind and agree with his beliefs
He will follow the rules you sell and take the decisions
you need

XXXVIII

Uneven

Where are the candles
Where are the black profile pics
Where are the protesters
Where are news channel crews

Does life value change with location
More for capital, less for small towns
If everyone's vote is equal
Then why "Anguish" is uneven

XXXIX
Selfish Needs

Don't wait for people to do the right thing
Most people lack courage and empathy
There is a reason why millions of kids sleep hungry
And actor's kid gets the front page

XL

Earth Is...

How self-obsessed we are
3/4 of the planet is Water
yet we call it Earth.

XLI

It's Up to You

You Never need a Reason to do the Right thing and
You can Always find an Excuse to do the Wrong

XLII

Weapon

Gun is easy, pen is heavy
One leaves trace on the ground
One leaves images in the mind
Both are potent, have pros and cons
Thank your God, I chose the latter one

XLIII

Don't Interfere

Let them laugh and smile
Their innocence won't last that long
Your world asks for being strong
Your will make these kids stop feeling at all

XLIV
Small Want

I am speechless, world moved on
It seems worthless, to carry on
I think it's senseless, to argue for
A chance of hope and a choice to stop

But in the midst, consider this
What made me a human without bliss
I just wanted, a small world
Of my love and a light to burn

XLV
Story

You are the reason that I exist
Your smile leads me to persist
This world can no longer resist
The story I wrote on time axis

XLVI

False Beliefs

How can you spot a demon
You don't know what it is
All you believe in is God
And still you doubt it

છ

Existence of one doesn't prove other
Logical fallacy is your best excuse
Stop pretending you do care
Child soldiers are the signs this point is true

XLVII

Sacrifice

I will win by Love and Compassion
I will rule in your loved one's hearts
I will be in your every angry moment
I will lose to you to make you human

XLVIII
Spilled Ink

Last time I acted, I wiped out a clan
I orchestrated a war, no blood left in their veins
I told the ways, how to fight the evil
Don't ask me again, to bring my pen of vengeance

XLIX
Light the Way

You are here and you are not
I am here but I am also lost

It's an existence I can't understand
I have you but I am alone

It feels good but also hurts a lot
You were right, we are all alone

So let me light a candle for us
And let the Light tell our story to rest

L
My Hell

I asked Death what's the deal
What to offer and what you mean
Tell me what you desire and need
I can sacrifice everything you heed

She told me I am too much to handle
I am a mess that hell can't saddle
You will be kept here to carry on
Your punishment is life with these morons

LI

See Us ALL

Quarantine might have taught something
How it feels to lose the freedom and liberty
What it means to live in fear
To see the protectors as people of danger

Hope you will realize the fear in Rwanda
What Yezidis faced and how Peshmerga pushed harder
Hope you will reconcile with the fact you denied
Your silence was the reason, millions cried and died

LII
Tables Turned

You think you pull the Strings
You think you make people Dance
You think you have the Choice
And you give people the Chance

But do you really feel in Control
Of threads you tightly hold
Do you think you are free from all
The Control you covet is my form

LIII

Pieces of Me

I am not my vacations, I am not my vocation
I am not what I keep on ignition
I am not my spouse and any relation
I am not my looks and reflection

I am just words, waiting for translation
I am just trust, my love's foundation
I am just a smile, stranger's affection
I am just a man, who once needed protection.

LIV
Pointless

Why challenge him
He doesn't want to fight
What chance do you have
He destroyed his "self"

LV

Good Man

There is something more than name
More than your money, more than fame
Kindness is a language that even animals understand
There is something above "Great", be a Good Man

LVI
Good Returns

Invest in Stocks, you Might get better return
Invest in People, you Might get Beautiful world

LVII

Core Truth

I may be broken but I am not weak
I may be confused but I remember the promise
I may be shattered but I will walk with you
I may be silent but my actions will be true

LVIII
The Teacher

It takes time to chisel a weapon
Time and pressure in right proportion,
Practice and persistence to train a warrior
To defeat the enemies outside and that lies interior

Then you need to leave the battleground
Let your student take the demons down
Your job is always to be the guide
That's the destiny of a teacher and time

LIX

Words to Inspire

Just another day, a thoughtful mile
Just another prayer, against mosaic tiles
Just another reason, to carry on
Just another poem, to make you smile

LX
Victory

I have seen how your world works
Against a woman and her will
You made the rules for your ego
I know the character of your ilk

But I know what you are scared of
It's her courage that you can't resist
Why would I have to fight you
She has already won, her old self no longer exists

LXI

Unknowing

It's dark to realize a heart alone
Love ain't eternal, like a prose
This journey is guided with unmarked stones
How can I fathom, what was mine, was another thorn

I saw the light, I tricked the shadows
How can I see now, the lines are shallow
I am blind by senses, but not by heart
I beat for longing, a long day of art

LXII

Mind's Eye

With every smile one realizes
The bliss comes from changed eyes
With different eyes come new vision
It changes perspective and distorted perception

LXIII

My Pack

I know my actions seem delayed
There is a reason, don't be dismayed
With the world running so fast, I get delayed
I have to pay the worthy, needy and the ones getting
trained

LXIV

See Me

I know I am harsh, sometimes unstable
I know I am uncertain, can't decide my flow
I know I have tried, but I am still on a "dose"
I just wish you feel, my soul is not sold

LXV

Illuminate

With Light you can Explore the Dark
With Dark you can Understand the Light

LXVI

Protectors

If you don't Respect a Soldier's sacrifice
Then don't Expect Relief when Evil strikes

LXVII
Virtual Dissenter

Long time ago, picked up virtual arms
Not just for chaos or order, but also for freelancing
charm
Lessons learnt were so sublime
Turned a simpleton into a warrior inside
Picked pen to declare my dissent
Waiting to send the message at the right Time

LXVIII

Guiding Light

If you face the Light
Darkness will fall behind
If you look for the Light
Darkness can be the guide

LXIX

Ultimate Cause

Sometimes people want their faith rewarded
They don't want all but few prayers deemed answered
It's not much to ask but the gestures
make a huge difference,
Sometimes Love is like interest, often compounded

I saw such love and tried to protect it
But I let go the war, to win the smaller battles
I see the view far from all this mess
My love is, has and will be true, it's time to confess

LXX

Two Ways

You saw a lot, I witnessed
You travelled a lot, I ventured
You experienced a lot, I immersed
You always thought of things other than you, I
submerged

LXXI

Gaslight

It's the "truths" I was told
Worse than lies that you believe
It's the "reality" I was sold
Worse than dreams that you see

It's the "help" that is given
Worse than wounds that you receive
It's the "love" that is shown
Worse than pain that you feel

It's the "support" that hurts
Worse than left alone on your own
It's the "light" that blinds
Worse than darkness just below

LXXII

Dance of Existence

With every count, learn the rhythm
With every rhythm, learn the motion
With every motion, learn the dance
With every dance, learn the existence

LXXIII

Row and Repeat

I see a boat on a sea
He waits for a wave, but they weigh heavy
In midst of this he realises time's tide
Why hide behind an excuse, let's row and repeat

FIND ME AT

Website - www.thebartendingpoet.com

Instagram - www.instagram.com/thebartendingpoet

Facebook - www.facebook.com/thebartendingpoet